Mothers are Everywhere

For Liz with thanks *K.W.*
For Stephanie and James *D.A.*

Mothers are Everywhere

Karen Wallace
Illustrated by David Axtell

OXFORD
UNIVERSITY PRESS

From the smallest mouse
to the biggest elephant,
every mother does her best
to look after her baby.

Mother elephants make a circle
when danger is near.
Baby elephants stay safe until
the danger is over.

Your mother makes a nursery
to keep you safe and warm.

A mother harvest mouse
lines her tiny nest with grass.
Her babies are warm
and safe, too.

Mothers give their babies milk
so they grow and grow
and grow.

Seal pups drink and drink.
Their mother's milk is extra rich.
They grow very fat, very fast,
to protect themselves from the cold.

Your mother tries her best to
give you food that you like.

A mother swan finds tender shoots
that are easy for her babies
to swallow.

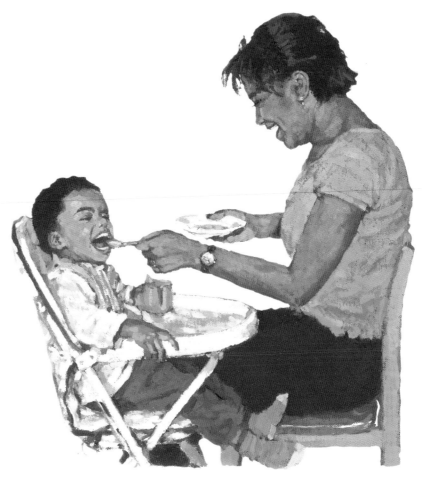

A mother chimpanzee teaches her baby
to use a stick to catch insects.

This baby thinks a spoon is
the best toy in the world.

Babies love bath time,
and keeping a baby clean is a full-time job.

This baby elephant is having a
shower to keep cool.
He doesn't care whether
he's clean or not.

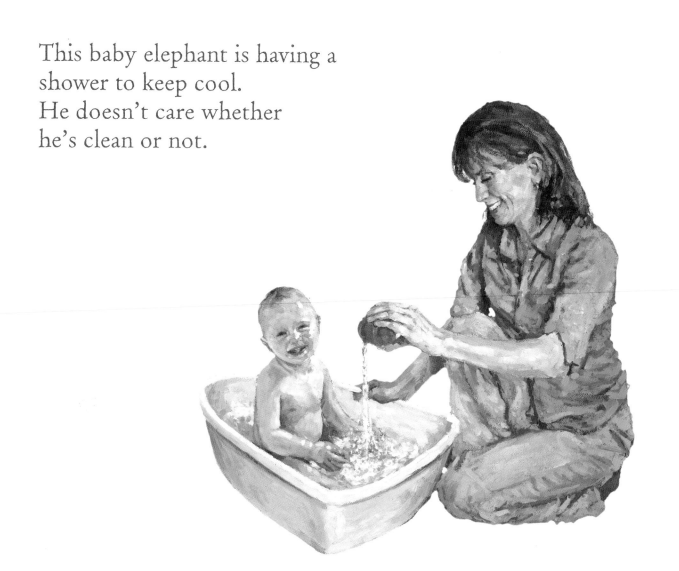

Mothers carry their babies to hold them close and keep them safe.

A mother orang-utan carries
her baby for more than two years.

Just as well her arms are powerful and strong!

A mother's voice is special.
Babies always know their mother's voice.

This mother dolphin makes
a clicking sound.
Her baby follows it from
the moment he's born.

All babies love water,
and they want to learn how to swim.
A mother teaches her baby
to swim on his own.

A baby otter needs to know how to swim,
so he can learn to catch fish.

Your mother loves to play
games with you.

Peek a boo!

A mother cheetah plays a game
to show her kittens how to hunt.

She twitches her tail ...
They chase it...
And pounce!

If a mother has to leave her baby,
she chooses someone she can trust.

Mother giraffes help one another
by looking after each other's babies.

Everyone needs a break sometimes!

Mothers must be sure to keep
their young ones safe.
Hold your mother's hand when
danger is near.

A baby shrew hangs
on to her mother.
Her brothers and sisters
hang on to each other.

Mothers hold their babies close
to help them go to sleep.
Tucked up in a mother's arms is
baby's favourite place to be!

Kittens can sleep peacefully
when their mother is
curled around them.

Some mothers have many babies.
Some only have one.
But all mothers do their best to
look after their babies.

Just like your mother looks after you!

Mothers are everywhere!

OXFORD
UNIVERSITY PRESS

Clarendon Street, Oxford OX2 6DP

Oxford University Press is a department of the University of Oxford.
It furthers the University's objective of excellence in research, scholarship,
and education by publishing worldwide in

Oxford New York

Athens Auckland Bangkok Bogotá Buenos Aires Calcutta
Cape Town Chennai Dar es Salaam Delhi Florence Hong Kong Istanbul
Karachi Kuala Lumpur Madrid Melbourne Mexico City Mumbai
Nairobi Paris São Paulo Singapore Taipei Tokyo Toronto Warsaw

with associated companies in Berlin Ibadan

Oxford is a registered trade mark of Oxford University Press
in the UK and in certain other countries

Text copyright © Karen Wallace 2001
Illustrations copyright © David Axtell 2001

The moral rights of the author and artist have been asserted

First published 2001

British Library Cataloguing in Publication Data available

Hardback   ISBN 0-19-279057-9
Paperback ISBN 0-19-272411-8

1 3 5 7 9 10 8 6 4 2

Printed in Hong Kong